HAL•LEONARD
INSTRUMENTAL
PLAY-ALONG

AUDIO ACCESS INCLUDED

PLAYBACK+
Speed • Pitch • Balance • Loop

CELLO

Gospel Hymns

Amazing Grace 2

Blessed Assurance 3

Down by the Riverside 4

He's Got the Whole World in His Hands 5

His Eye Is on the Sparrow 6

In the Garden 7

Leaning on the Everlasting Arms 8

The Old Rugged Cross 9

Precious Memories 10

Shall We Gather at the River? 11

Sweet By and By 12

There Is Power in the Blood 13

Wayfaring Stranger 14

When We All Get to Heaven 15

Whispering Hope 16

To access audio visit:
www.halleonard.com/mylibrary

Enter Code
8434-1514-2641-0887

ISBN 978-1-4950-7388-5

HAL•LEONARD®
7777 W. BLUEMOUND RD. P.O. BOX 13819 MILWAUKEE, WI 53213

In Australia Contact:
Hal Leonard Australia Pty. Ltd.
4 Lentara Court
Cheltenham, Victoria, 3192 Australia
Email: ausadmin@halleonard.com.au

Visit Hal Leonard Online at
www.halleonard.com

AMAZING GRACE

CELLO

Words by JOHN NEWTON
Traditional American Melody

BLESSED ASSURANCE

Lyrics by FANNY J. CROSBY
Music by PHOEBE PALMER KNAPP

CELLO

DOWN BY THE RIVERSIDE

CELLO

African American Spiritual

HE'S GOT THE WHOLE WORLD IN HIS HANDS

CELLO

Traditional Spiritual

HIS EYE IS ON THE SPARROW

CELLO

Words by CIVILLA D. MARTIN
Music by CHARLES H. GABRIEL

IN THE GARDEN

CELLO

Words and Music by
C. AUSTIN MILES

LEANING ON THE EVERLASTING ARMS

CELLO

Words by ELISHA A. HOFFMAN
Music by ANTHONY J. SHOWALTER

THE OLD RUGGED CROSS

CELLO

Words and Music by
REV. GEORGE BENNARD

PRECIOUS MEMORIES

CELLO

Words and Music by
J.B.F. WRIGHT

SHALL WE GATHER AT THE RIVER?

CELLO

Words and Music by
ROBERT LOWRY

SWEET BY AND BY

CELLO

Words by SANFORD FILLMORE BENNETT
Music by JOSEPH P. WEBSTER

THERE IS POWER IN THE BLOOD

CELLO

Words and Music by
LEWIS E. JONES

WAYFARING STRANGER

CELLO

Southern American Folk Hymn

WHEN WE ALL GET TO HEAVEN

Words by ELIZA E. HEWITT
Music by EMILY D. WILSON

CELLO

WHISPERING HOPE

CELLO

Words and Music by
ALICE HAWTHORNE